The LION ROARS

TEN SERMONS FROM MARK FOR THE LENTEN SEASON

ARTHUR H. KOLSTI

C.S.S. Publishing Company
Lima, Ohio

THE LION ROARS

5804/ISBN 0-89536-720-3

PRINTED IN U.S.A.

Table of Contents

To Josée

Introduction

Current scholarship on Mark's gospel is one of the exciting frontiers in New Testament study. Rediscovery of the first gospel reveals why the traditional symbol for Mark is a lion. He roars through his story telling.

Through the years I have naturally assumed that the gospels were written to tell the story of Jesus to the world at large. A new look at Mark leads to the conclusion that they were also written to help *the church* get the story straight. Mark was a reformer of the church and, along with all the gospel writers, is engaged in an ongoing lover's quarrel with the church.

The pastor who would uncover a host of new insights for preaching is urged to begin a journey of rediscovery through the gospels. Mark is a fitting place to begin, for both Matthew and Luke use him as a source, weaving in their own subtle variations.

In such a journey the main source is the text itself. The first step is to read and reread Mark making one's own outline, notes, and observations. Then the study can proceed to commentaries and other Markan literature. The annotated bibliography lists resources I have found to be of high value as helps in moving beyond exegesis to interpretation.

Bon Voyage!

— Arthur H. Kolsti

Ash Wednesday

Mark 1:21-28

Crazy In One Language, Sane In Another

Those of you who take up the challenge to read the Gospel of Mark will observe that one of his literary techniques is to tell a story within a story, that one might reinforce and interpret the other. I'm going to copy Mark's style and start this sermon by telling you a true story. The story was told originally by a pastoral counselor who was for many years the senior chaplain of a large state mental hospital. One of his saddest cases was a schizophrenic Greek, hopelessly out of touch with reality. He was a sad "back ward" case who had been vegetating in the hospital for years. No one quite knew where this patient had come from. But everybody agreed that nothing could be done for him, so no one paid much attention to him. The chaplain finally arranged for a local Greek Orthodox priest to visit the poor fellow. Aside from pastoral reasons, the chaplain thought the visit would at least give the patient a chance to talk to someone in his native language. He hadn't been able to do that for years.

The priest, who was also a competent counselor, returned from the visit quite shaken ans asked the chaplain, "What on earth is that fellow doing here? He's as healthy as you and I." They did some research and by bits and pieces put together the man's story. The Greek schizophrenic was a sailor who had jumped ship long ago in a nearby port. He spoke no English. Somehow he got into trouble and, as sometimes happens when our system miscarries, he was clapped into the mental hospital. There in the hospital he slowly learned English. But he learned his English from other schizophrenic patients. One frequent characteristic of this particular mental dysfunction is a certain misuse of lanquage. The poor Greek sailor managed to learn completely schizophrenic language. To the English-speaking doctors he in fact sounded and acted schizophrenic and was every bit as removed from reality as the sickest of his fellow patients.

The Greek Orthodox priest had conversed with him in Greek, something that had never happened before in the hospital. When he spoke in his native language, the man was absolutely normal.

There you have the story: crazy in English, sane in Greek. Language and reality are intertwined. Language is the way we express the reality we experience.

In the case of the Greek sailor two different languages were spoken to reveal his two different realities, his two different "worlds." We can understand how the confusion occurred; Greek for one world: English for another world.

The remarkable incident in Mark adds a compounding element. Jesus and his hearers are both speaking the *same* language, but there are two "worlds," two realities, two experiences represented. We all have had a disagreement with someone, and, although speaking the same language, we say, "We are not speaking the same language." Coming from different points of reference, different points of view, different realities, words can convey opposite meanings. When that happens, in frustration, we say to our opponents, "You're crazy."

Jesus came speaking a "language" foreign to his adversaries. To understand his words required an upside-down mentality which calls evil good and good evil, light darkness and darkness light, bitter sweet and sweet bitter. Little wonder the critics of Jesus called him a madman.

How illuminating all this is as we focus on Mark's account of the opening of Jesus' ministry. If you want to think of the world as one big insane asylum, you will not be far from the New Testament diagnosis of the human condition. And, it's not too difficult to think that way about the world in view of much of the history we have lived through in this twentieth century. To talk of Jesus casting out demons is just a first century way of witnessing to him as the one who comes to restore wholeness and sanity to a world touched by madness. Jesus comes to challenge the distorted reading of reality which can capture institutions and individuals. That challenge eventually cost him his life.

How does Jesus challenge the world's madness? With a flip of his hand? With an incantation? With some words of mumbo jumbo? Those were the stock in trade approach among first century exorcists. Jesus comes to talk to us, to initiate a conversation, to speak to us in the language of God, our native language. Yes, it's our native language. We are not unlike the Greek sailor. We are exiles, exiles from Eden. And we have been taught to think and speak in the language of this world.

The vocabulary of love runs counter to the vocabulary this world so often teaches. If you saw *South Pacific,* you will remember the song, Carefully Taught. The song reminds us how those around us insist on carefully teaching us all their inherited biases and prejudices.

Jesus comes to teach. That's one of Mark's favorite titles for Jesus, teacher. Jesus enters the Synagogue at Capernaum to teach. He begins in the household of God. A man is sitting in the synagogue who has an unclean spirit. Madness is in the world and the world's madness gets into the church. The demon is cast out. The man is made whole. The people ask, "What is this, a new teaching?" The question seems strange. Mark wants it made quite clear *that it is the power and authority of the words of Jesus that restore sanity.* Jesus is not the itinerant wonder worker dispensing a string of benefits. He comes to engage the human community in conversation.

During the darkest days of the Battle of Britain, people in Britain and people beyond Britain were sustained by the words of Winston Churchill; the sound of a man's voice. Someone has said of Churchill's wartime speeches: "He mobilized the English language and sent it into battle." Enlarge the thought and apply it to Jesus. "He mobilized the language of God and sent it into battle." I think so. Mark would like that. Mark's other favored title for Jesus is Son of Man, a title which enshrines the church's conviction that the words and actions of Jesus bear the stamp of the full moral authority of God. Jesus is the agent of our liberation. He mobilizes the language of God and takes it into battle.

And it is a battle! The man was not healed without a convulsion. Here is another true story that has in it echoes of the incident at Capernaum. A friend of mine was preaching in a West Coast Congregation. His text was the words of Jesus: "Blessed are the peacemakers." In the middle of the sermon, the commander of a local veterans organization stood up, shook his fist at the preacher, and strode angrily out of the church. Shades of Capernaum. "What do you have to do with us, have you come to destroy us, Jesus of Nazareth?" "Leave war to the generals, economics to the business men, and government to the politicians." The Word is engaged in struggle. The Word sifts as well as binds, threatens as well as promises. The word is now introduced into the human dialogue.

Crazy in one language, sane in another. Where is sanity? Is it in the words that describe a dense pack of MX missiles as "The Peacekeepers," or is it in the words of him who cried over Jerusalem, "You know not the things that make for peace."

Where is sanity? Does it reside in the teaching of worldly wisdom, "take care of number one," or does it reside in the words, "whoever loses his life for my sake and the Gospel's will find his life."

Where is sanity? In the words of consumerism, racism, terrorism, self-indulgence? Or does sanity dwell in the words of Jesus of Nazareth? The world called him a madman and fashioned a cross for him. The empire struck back.

In the closing line of Masefield's play, *Good Friday,* a woman standing by the cross as Jesus dies says to the centurion: "Where do you think he is now?" The centurion replies: "Let loose in the world, lady, where neither Roman nor Jew can stop his truth: And in our world, wherever the Gospel is proclaimed, the Word goes forth to battle for the sake of sanity.

Lent 1

Mark 1:35-45

A Ministry of Interruptions

When I just read you the account of Jesus healing the leper and substituted the word anger for the word pity, I was not taking capricious liberty nor presuming to rewrite scripture. The change has behind it the authority of the most ancient manuscripts which use the Greek word "orgistheis"..."anger." That Jesus was angry is also supported by the words used later in the account "and he sternly charged him." The Greek word translated sternly means literally "snorting." Jesus was wrought up with anger and irritation as he charged the leper to say nothing but simply present himself to the priests according to Levitical Law.

We stumble over the word anger. It bumps up against some of our pious sentiments about Jesus. Maybe Mark is bringing us face to face with a quite human Jesus, a Jesus just as human as we are. The third support for the use of the word anger is the testimony of our own experience. Just think of the way you sometimes feel when you are suddenly interrupted; interrupted in a way that imposes upon you an inconvenience, a diversion from your carefully planned agenda. I don't mean just any kind of interruption. All of us can easily hang up on the telephone caller who interrupts us just as we're walking out the door with a spiel about a discount offer for magazine subscriptions. I mean the kind of interruption calling for a response on our part to a valid human need. That is precisely the situation Jesus was in.

He had just opened his public ministry. He was anxious to get about the task of establishing his authority in the towns of Galilee. Even before sun-up he called his disciples to fall in. "Let us go on to the next towns that I may preach there also for that is why I was called." So he started out and had a few early encounters, a few sermons delivered, a few twisted minds made whole. Then just as he's getting into his mission (and he really wanted it to be a preaching ministry primarily) this leper appears in front of him. "If you will, you can make me clean."

It will help us to remember that lepers were not just called sick. They were called unclean, unholy, polluted. They were morally condemned by the guardians of God's truth, those who presume to put everyone in their proper slot. You heard the Levitical instructions. Lepers were isolated, made to dress in rags with the upper lip covered, forced to warn others off with the cry, "unclean, unclean." To draw near to Jesus took something special on the part of this particular leper. He was risking being driven away by stones. There must have been some shred of human dignity left within him to make him rebel against his condition.

And the leper's presence posed a special problem for Jesus. No, do not think for a moment there is any doubt about the way Jesus will respond, or at least should respond. He is under divine constraint. He is the son of the living God whose love reaches out even to the furthest outposts of the humanly profane and unclean. Jesus reached out and touched the man, "I will; be clean." And in doing that, Jesus created a problem for himself. It meant he had to abort his plans to go on to other towns. With that touch centuries of prejudice were assaulted. With that touch a challenge was thrown out to the priestly guardians of holiness. "Show yourself to the priests and keep your mouth shut." How could the priests acknowledge the cure without acknowledging the curer. "And after you've seen the priests, continue to keep your mouth shut." After all, anyone who touched a leper became himself polluted, ceremonially impure. The gates of every town in Galilee would be officially closed to Jesus. Jesus, knowing what would happen, tried to salvage the situation by telling the man to keep his lips sealed. But, the man talked all over the place, and it was as Jesus knew it would be. "He could no longer enter a town openly." Mission aborted by an untimely interruption. But listen, there's an unexpected twist. Mark observes: "He was out in the country and people came to him from every quarter." Is this a word to us about the cross and crown, about the shape of our own calling as Christians and vocation as a church? Maybe there is such a thing as a ministry of interruptions.

Now I want to share with you something from my own experience that helps me to understand the emotions of Jesus in this incident. I arrived in Topeka, Kansas, in 1963 as the new minister of a central city church. We were not there long before the whole civil rights movement picked up steam and touched every city in America. People marched in the streets. Issues of judgment and fairness were being raised. The atmosphere was volatile and emotional. Our associate minister went off and marched at Selma and that upset a lot of people. Community groups were forming around the issue of civil rights and asking the clergy, especially of the major churches in town, to lend their presence publicly. "If you will, you can help us."

I really had no problems with those whose vocation it was to represent the Gospel in the world. I really had no doubts about where those of us who preach the Gospel ought to stand. But I confess to having been angry with the civil rights movement and wrought up by these calls for advocacy coming from various quarters of the community. As far as I was concerned, none of this was coming at the right time for me. I was new in Central Church; I needed time to become known, to get my feet on the ground, to build a following. I didn't want to be thrown a hot potato, interrupted by a controversial issue. I knew something about the flack that could be expected. I would become unacceptable to some.

My emotions were wrought up. I remembered how Jesus reached out across walls to touch people. I resolved my feelings and made my decision by writing a little poem — not good poetry; just a poem in which I tried to express my thinking process at the time. I have never shared it before, I share it with you now. It is entitled "Hands"

The hands of Christ were loving hands
That stooped to touch the spittle and the clay.
The hands of Christ were serving hands
That drew not back from human need.
The hands of Christ were wounded hands
that counted not the cost.

And yet, you say, "take heed
Keep distant from their kind
And keep them in their place."

Or else you counsel prudence
For self must care for self.
But, Oh, those hands again appear
Tinted with grime and sweat and blood.
You cannot argue with those hands
Doubt not, they say, "My name is Love."

And that in essence is the Gospel message to church and world. God's name is love, Christlike love, cruciform in shape. And knowing that some interruptions can alter your way, what else can you do when confronted with human need, if you are indeed under the constraint of Jesus Christ, the Word of the living God? I wonder if Mark didn't use this particular story of Jesus and the leper to say something primarily to Christians, not only in his own day, but in every day. Did Mark see within the church of his day, a young church just starting out, a tendency to hang on the door a sign reading "Do Not Disturb?" What about the church today and some of the issues seeking advocacy..."If you will, you can make a difference."

In the communications crossing my desk from city ministries there is a new tone, a tone of urgency. Human problems in our nation and world are escalating. The human hurt in the cities is getting worse. What if we allow ourselves to reach out more and more to the untouchables of this world? What then, Mark says: "They came to him from every quarter." Dare we read him to say: Let the word go out that the church really cares, that the church can be interrupted by the cry for help, and people who think the church does not care will come to it again?

And since the Gospel is finally a personal word to each one of us, this story from Mark speaks to us individually as well as collectively. Plumb your own memory and recall someone who responded to an interruption from you: some teacher who went out of his or her way to help you get back on the track; someone you may have hardly known who heard your call..."If you will you can help me," and that someone helped you.

Think of the interruptions which can break into your day, in the light of your calling to follow Christ. Listen to these words of a professor at Notre Dame. "You know, my whole life I have been complaining that my work was constantly interrupted, until I discovered that my interruptions were my work." If I understand correctly the point Mark is making, that is the way it is for someone who responds to the call of Christ. Perhaps through this story of Jesus and the leper, the risen Lord is calling you to reach out in some new and risky way. If we abort our plans and follow him, what then? Peter asked that question of Jesus, and Jesus said "You will find mothers and fathers, brothers and sisters," a caring family. That's not a bad exchange.

Lent 2

Mark 2:1-12

The Great Break Out

The story in this selection from Mark's Gospel is one that begins with a break in and ends with a break out. It's a dramatic sequence of events. Jesus is at home in Capernaum. Whose home? According to Mark, Jesus' home. Matthew and Luke lead us to believe Jesus had no home specifically his own. Many scholars stumble over this verse. Oh, they say it really must have been Peter's home and Mark is confused. But Mark doesn't say it was somebody else's home. According to Mark, Jesus maintained a bachelor pad. Maybe he did. Why not? It gets wearing to be a perpetual house guest. Why shouldn't Jesus have a place where he could kick off his sandals and not always have to act like the preacher come to dinner, or listen to his family complain about the company he was starting to keep — tax collectors and sinners? Why is it so difficult to think of Jesus in a human way?

According to Mark, Jesus was at home by himself. But then someone spotted a light in the window, smoke in the chimney or something. And word got out that he was at home. They came from all over, intruded right into his privacy and turned his house into a meeting hall. In fact, so many showed up, they were jammed into the hallway and filling up the front yard. Homes and synagogues were becoming impossible places for Jesus to hold forth. Crowd control was becoming a problem.

On the fringes of the crowd there was a man who desperately wanted to see Jesus. He was a paralytic, immobile. He couldn't even stand up, let alone walk. And even if he could have it would take at least the front line of the Washington Redskins to run interference for him. But he had four friends who cared about him very much. They were convinced that Jesus could help him. They climbed up on the roof, got the paralytic up there too, stretcher and all. Then they started scraping and chipping away.

Soon they had a hole large enough to let the man down, pallet and all. They really wrecked the roof. I wonder if they ever got a bill for its repairs. Jesus was overwhelmed when the scenario unfolded before him. Mark says, "When he saw their faith," he said to the man, "Son, your sins are forgiven." They hadn't brought him there for that; they wanted him healed. And if he is forgiven, why can't he walk now. The piety of the day said that if you sin, God will punish you by making you sick, or blind, or deaf, or handicapped. This story breaks that deadly connection. It was time to challenge that lie, time for people to stop thinking of God as the cosmic jailer. The man was still on his stretcher while the conversation shifted to Jesus and the Scribes. The Scribes were shocked because they had just witnessed an act of blasphemy, a mere man presuming to stand in the place of God, and do what only God can do. The charge was in the air that would eventually help put Jesus on the cross.

Jesus sensed the thoughts of his critics and posed a question to them. "Which is easier to say to the paralytic, 'Your sins are forgiven' or 'Rise, take up your pallet and walk.' " Neither one is any magician's trick. The Greek word translated rise is the same word used in the Gospel for resurrection. Which is easier, to forgive sins or give the gift of new life? Only God can do either. Then Jesus delivered the bombshell. He declared himself to be the human face of God in history. "That you may know, that the Son of Man on earth has authority to forgive sins, I say to you 'Rise, take up your pallet and walk.' "

It is necessary for us at this point to look at that title, Son of Man. It would be a title familiar to everyone in that house. According to the dominant religious outlook of that day, everything would stay as it was until God decided to ring down the curtain on human history. At that time he would send his agent, a resplendent more-than-human figure called the Son of Man. There would be a general resurrection. The Son of Man would reward the righteous and confirm their place in the new order. The sinners, he would send off to everlasting destruction. He would conquer the gentile nations and destroy all who did not acknowledge the preeminence of Israel and accept her definitions of the way things are. The Son of Man was a very destructive figure, a cosmic hit man for God and his saints. Forgiveness was not in his portfolio. But here was Jesus, a Galilean carpenter, presuming to act on God's behalf, forgiving sins and restoring a "sinner" to the community of faith.

Listen to these words from a book entitled *Enoch,* one widely read in the days of Jesus. The writer is talking about the day of the Son of Man. "And the righteous and elect shall be saved on that day, and they shall never henceforth see the face of sinners and the unrighteous." Heaven was going to be a special place for a very few people. Some folk have that kind of blinders-in-place world view.

> *Even up in heaven*
> *She believes that little black cherubs*
> *Rise at seven to do celestial chores*
> *while her class lies late in bed*
> *and snores.*

> *— Anonymous*

When the paralytic was on his feet, Jesus told him to go home. He would be quite visible to the righteous, walking around in his village. Jesus was giving them a preview of what God was really up to in history, and in the process, Jesus was turning their world upside down. Of course, in Mark's eyes Jesus was putting God's world right side up.

This was a very different kind of Son of Man. Jesus redefined the meaning of the title. He reached back into the Prophets of Israel. Ezekiel, for example, used the title of himself. "Son of Man, stand upon your feet and I will speak to you." "He spoke" says Ezekiel "And his spirit entered into me." Ezekiel used the phrase to enshrine the mystery of the God who is not alien to our humanness. He meets us within the world, shares his spirit, and gives us his life-giving Word. In the process he makes himself vulnerable. We can reject that Word, spit it out of our mouth, turn upon the word bearer.

And here, if you will, is how I would phrase the Gospel witness to us in calling Jesus the Son of Man. For us, the man, Jesus, is a parable of the character and purpose of the Living God, the God who himself breaks into the human predicament, that we might break out. Mark reports, "They were astonished." The Greek words suggest some sort of emotional movement in their heads. We would say the whole thing blew their minds.

Now I want to use a good Markan tecnique and tell another story to illumine the Gospel story. There was a film currently showing in Boston at the Exeter Theatre. *Yol* is a Turkish story about modern Turkey, a film made at considerable risk. The background is a nation which is a virtual prison: rigid, paralyzed, suffocating. Not just politically imprisoned but bound also by custom, tradition and religion. One reinforces the other. The story centers on three political prisoners who are granted leave from prison to visit their homes. The experience of one is instructive. When he gets home, he is told his wife is at her father's house in disgrace. She deserted the family when her husband went to prison and was discovered working in a brothel. Her family retrieved her. They put her in a dingy room, chained her feet, forbade her to bathe and fed her bread and water. By the time her husband got leave from prison she had been held thus for eight months.

The prisoner's brother tells him that this insult to family honor must be avenged and if he does not want to kill his wife, the brothers will do what custom dictates. The prisoner says he will go retrieve his son and punish her by death. It is winter, severe winter. He must travel the treacherous mountain pass to his wife's village. The land is locked in ice and snow as the people are locked in their inflexible traditions sanctioned by a God who issues inflexible decrees.

He finds his wife at her family home. He cannot find it within himself to use a knife. He decides that she can follow him and his son back across the treacherous mountain pass, knowing she will probably not survive the trip. At mid journey she collapses in the snow. He keeps moving on. His young son points to her floundering and asks the father: "If you wanted her dead, why did you let her come with us?" The prisoner goes back, the wife is pleading, "Forgive me, forgive me." He hesitates, then places her on his back and resumes the tortuous journey. One senses that his human act of forgiveness is a dramatic moment. An inflexible tradition which defines the way things are and have to be has been breached. There is a breaking out of a vicious cycle and *forgiveness* is the key. A New possibility for restored human community is in the air.

The travelers arrive at the village, but it is too late. The wife dies from exposure; the prisoner returns to prison; but you sense that even though still a prisoner, he just might be, in a deeper sense, free. In the film story the act of forgiveness is the one sign of hope.

Where does the break out begin? It begins with the inbreaking of a new style. We are coming close to the Gospel of the Son of Man who comes to us in history as one of us to extend the promise of the Living God; "Your sins are forgiven." And how often we have heard the words. Do we believe them? Do we let them tie up with our own inner load of remembered failures, the gnawing sense that maybe we haven't brought life off just the way we should have. Your sins are forgiven! Faith is our acceptance of God's acceptance of us.

But it doesn't end there with personal forgiveness. It's not just some kind of private transaction between the individual and God. The gift is followed by the command, rise and walk as a contributing part of the restored humanity of God. Who is the paralytic? Certainly the man brought to Jesus. But, to the imaginative eye, who is he? Can he be first-century Israel bound by a crippling piety and a suffocating tradition that freezes the possibilities of human community? Can he be any nation or group locked into a spiritual dystrophy by ideology or culture? Can he be you or I, feeling impotent before powers that seem to defy human control, bound by guilty memories, impeded by hang ups, caught in a human relations bind of our own making? What is the key to breaking out? What is the key to new possibilities of human community and individual action? We have the authoritative answer of the Son of Man. "Your sins are forgiven." You, forgive one another as God has forgiven you.

When does new possibility arise in a marriage that is in a bind? Isn't it when wife can say to husband and husband to wife, "forgive me my offenses against you." Where do new possibilities emerge in a polarized world, new possibilities between Protestant, Catholic, Jew and Arab, white and black and brown and yellow, American and Russian and we could go on and on. The new possibility emerges when within each group the words begin to form, "forgive us our trespasses against you."

In Jesus' house in Capernaum there is a sign of hope for a petrified age. Both cross and resurrection are foreshadowed in the story. It's still a cold, rigid world outside the doors, but one man has at least broken out of the deadly paralysis through an encounter with the inbreaking Son of Man.

There is a scene in one of Isaac Asimov's science fiction stories that bears on our theme. Daneel Olivaw is the prince of robots. He has had certain "laws of Justice programmed into him." A man named Elijah has remained human and fallible and tells Daneel the story of the woman taken in adultery.

Daneel responds, "What is adultery?"

"That doesn't matter. It is a crime for which the accepted punishment was stoning."

"And the woman was guilty?"

"She was."

"Then why was she not stoned?" Daneel asks.

"None of the accusers felt he could after Jesus' statement. The story is meant to show there is something even higher than the justice you have been filled with, Daneel. There is human impulse known as mercy, a human act known as forgiveness."

"I am not acquainted with these words, partner Elijah."*

That is a gruesome concept of the world of tomorrow. A human impulse known as mercy, a human act known as forgiveness. These are the final realities which if lost from the human vocabulary will certainly mean the end of man and the end of new alternatives to the old cycle of punch and counter punch. Over against this gruesome vision here are some words the church inscribed over the story of Jesus.

Through the tender mercy of our God
Whereby the Dayspring from on high has visited us
To give light to them that sit in darkness
and in the shadow of death
And to guide our feet in the way of peace.

Lent 3
Mark 5:1-20

The Man Named Legion

They begged him to leave. They were polite enough about it, but the message was plainly there, "Jesus, go home." According to Mark's itinerary, he had taken his first step into Gentile territory. But, lest we think the vested interests here will be any less upset by his presence then the vested interests in Israel, we are soon disabused of any such notion. Vested interests are the same everywhere. They are easily threatened by change. This rejection of Jesus on Gentile turf foreshadows his rejection by Gentile power brokers as well as those in Israel. When he reaches the end of his increasingly lonely road, it will be Gentile soldiers who will pound the nails into his hands.

Review the incident that led to this confrontation. They get out of their little boat after being battered by wind and wave on the sea of Galilee. They're in foreign territory now. That fact alone might make the disciples a bit uneasy. What they encounter would make anyone uneasy, a lunatic coming out of the cemetery. Cemeteries in those days were often the places where distraught people found refuge in the caves that served as crypts. This man was particularly violent, a danger to himself and others. A volcanic rage seethed within him. We would probably call him a manic depressive. People then said he had an unclean spirit; he was possessed by a demon — same reality, different vocabulary.

The Gerasene way of responding to human disorder is evident

in the text: "For he had often been bound with fetters and chains, but the chains he wrenched apart, and the fetters he broke in pieces: and no one had the strength to subdue him." That word subdue should more properly be rendered "tame." "No one could *tame* him." Tame, that's something you do to an animal. This man was the object of a chains and fetters policy, a dehumanizing policy. It was a zoo keeper's mentality that dealt with human wretchedness in the land of the Gerasenes. You can call it an extreme law-and-order approach. But it wasn't working very well.

And did you catch the way the man spoke to Jesus? "I adjure you by God, do not torment me." He runs up to Jesus and pleads that the Son of God not hurt him. Suppose you crossed a stranger's path and the first thing he said to you was "Please don't hurt me." The hurting kind was evidently the only kind of human encounter this man had ever experienced. He's been brutalized by people. No wonder he's like a volcano ready to blow his top at any moment, all that pressure from accumulated hurts and resentment. Some folk have only known these sorts of human encounters from childhood up.

I find the story beginning to intersect left and right with ongoing human experience. I knew a police chief once who understood his vocation as that of a zoo keeper. He didn't put it in those words, but that's how it came out. He was right in insisting that you can't let violence run loose, but what he lacked was an understanding of the brutalizing effect on people of poverty and prejudice and injustice, an effect that stokes the fires of the human volcano. You just cannot go on keeping the lid on things without addressing the conditions which brutalize people and turn a city into a potential disaster area. Nor can you expect to see the zoo keeper policy work when applied to the global village.

Make no mistake; Jesus was taking a risk in approaching this man. The man could hurt him. Jesus was vulnerable. But Jesus was committed to human encounters of another kind. Not the kind that brutalize and make for alienation and sickness. But the humanizing kind that creates opportunities for community and wholeness. "What is your name?" Jesus asks the man. "Tell me about yourself." "My name is Legion," he replies, "for we are many." A legion is a Roman military unit of about 6,000 men. The man obviously has an identity problem. Maybe he's identifying with the Roman overlords. Maybe he thought he was Julius Caesar swaggering around out there in the tombs. That can happen; you can become like your oppressors; the psychiatrists call it "introjection."

But I think he really was many people. All of us are. What is your name? What is my name? I think of the man who said: "I'm not a person; I'm a committee." There is a sense in which all of us are named legion. I find a great deal of affinity with these words by E. S. Martin:

> *Within my earthly temple there's a crowd*
> *There's one of us that's humble, one that's proud*
> *There's one that's broken hearted for his sins,*
> *There's one who unrepentant sits and grins;*
> *There's one who loves his neighbors as he loves himself.*
> *There's one who cares for naught but fame and self.*
> *From such corroding cares I would be free.*
> *If once I could determine which is me.*
> *My name is Legion.*

Suddenly the incident begins to intersect with personal experience. Maybe discovering our true selves is the most important enterprise in life. And we will see that this man has his identity problem resolved through this encounter with Jesus.

But before Mark does that he adds a strange twist to the story. The demons beg Jesus to let them enter a herd of swine. Jesus gives them leave to do so, but despite their own wishes for survival, the demons impel the swine into a suicidal plunge into the sea of Galilee. If you do not believe the scholars and commentators get all tied up talking about this bizarre bit about the pigs, believe me, they do. Some just write it off as a bit of superstitious folklore which became attached to the tradition. So no commentary has anything of help for the interpreter of this passage.

But I note this; this is a detail Matthew and Luke both preserve in their accounts of the incident, though they modify other parts of the story. I also have too much respect for the sophistication of the Gospel writers. All three not only keep the incident; they preface this episode with the story of the stilling of the storm at sea. I see a larger reference here. The disciples who follow Jesus on the sea are saved. The demons perish in the same sea. Remember, the sea in biblical tradition is a rich metaphor for the volatile currents of history. The suicidal plunge of the pigs becomes a sign of the doom of the demonic. The picture of the herd driven by hysteria is an unforgettable one. Many of you watched the "Winds of War." You saw again old film clips of goose-stepping SS batallions marching along to the cheers of an hysterial nation. The picture of the suicidal pigs is not without its significance for any community driven by the demons of greed, arrogance, gluttony, insensitivity, the passions of the blood and mind.

But back to the story. In the closing scenes, we find the man sitting at the feet of Jesus, clothed and in his right mind. He has assumed the position of discipleship, sitting, listening, learning. He's hearing some words now that have within them the power to make sense out of life. It's a beautiful scene and it's contemporary history wherever and whenever it happens.

But the delegation from the Chamber of Commerce arrives. When they see the scene, they are afraid. They were more comfortable with the old arrangements. Of course, there has been a property loss and that could score heavily with them. Maybe they count pigs as more important than people. Whatever, they evidently prefer to be part of the old problems rather than participants in new solutions. Those who today can only think in terms of the nuclear madness tell us the other alternatives are risky. For one thing, military contracts mean jobs. Suicidal policies might mean a world destroyed, but that is not mentioned. New alternatives might create new economic opportunities; that's not mentioned. The citizens of the land of the Gerasenes understand the power of vested interests and the persuasiveness of the logic of insanity. They beg Jesus to leave. He has made himself vulnerable again. These solid townsfolk, they too can hurt him. In fact they could be even more dangerous. It is one thing to cope with madness as it thrashes around in the tombs. It is quite another thing to deal with madness when it wears the robes of respectability. I recall the words of a Black leader who said: "I'm not worried about the Klansmen who run around the countryside in white sheets and burn crosses. I can see them. It's the ones I can't recognize that worry me — the ones who wear three-piece suits and sit in the board rooms of banks and corporations." These are the ones who can really hurt. Jesus goes back to the boat; the man once named Legion begs that he might come along. Once he didn't want Jesus near him; now he doesn't want to leave him. Now instead, it's the good solid citizens who don't want Jesus in their midst.

Jesus commissions the man as an apostle to his own people. You do not have to be near the earthly Jesus to be his servant and story teller. And that's good news for us Gentiles who are called to be his men and women in the here and now. To be the Lord's man or the Lord's woman is to be found by the identity who brings order to our own legion-like lives.

In the last resort the Gospel is always personal. Mark's story has given us another glimpse of the Lord of liberation and life as he moves into history. And the bottom line is the wonderful things that happen in these fragmented lives of ours when we begin to listen to this man; when he gets inside of us and starts rearranging the furniture in our heads; when his love, his royal claim, his serving purpose take over.

Lent 4

Mark 7:31-37

The Recovery of Voice

In the confirmation rite of the ancient church there is a moment when the priest moistens his finger with saliva and makes the sign of the cross on the forehead of the confirmed. The practice is rooted in the church's memory of the action of Jesus with the man who could neither hear nor speak. It is Mark who preserves this memory and in his account we are as close to the historic Jesus as we can be anywhere in the gospel. One word is especially significant, "ephphatha," the liberating command to ears and tongue. It's an Aramaic word and the fact it stayed in the tradition as an Aramaic word says something about its impact on the early church.

Mark preserves three such words in the tradition. The first is the intimate word "Abba," "Father," on the lips of Jesus in prayer. The second is the word that raises a little girl from death — "Talithi Cumi," "Little girl, arise, stand up." The third is the word that makes possible human communication, "Ephphatha," "be opened." Think, three words that are distinctive to being human, more than just an animal. "Abba," "Father," the word points us to the distinctive human dimension. We are addressed by God and in turn can address him. "Talithi Cumi," "rise," "stand up"; the distinctive human posture, the posture separating us from all the four-footed creatures. "To stand before God" in biblical imagery is the posture of human dignity. It is interesting to note the word "rise" or "stand up" is the same word used in speaking of resurrection. It suggests our ultimate destiny is to stand before God. "Ephphatha," "be opened," to be able to communicate the distinctive human capacity. What on earth is Jesus up to then and now? He comes to enable us to be what God wanted us to be in the first place, truly human in all that distinctive word means.

Think of the power of speech, the capacity which opens up all sorts of human possibilities. At some point in our development as a species, we were given the power to communicate. A voice to the voiceless, the gift distinctively human. A voice to the voiceless that says the gospel is part of the miracle of God's love in human lives. Can you or I imagine what it means to be mute, voiceless, dumb? It means isolation. It means being spoken to, spoken for, spoken about, but never speaking. It means getting along by signs and grunts. You can never ask a question, never protest, never affirm. You are locked up with your own surging emotions. Without the power of words, there is no bridge for you into human community. In the end, being mute means being ignored, stereotyped, passed by. It can mean unjust treatment at hands of police or the system of criminal justice. Deaf and voiceless people have been shot because they did not hear a police order to halt or because their sounds and gestures were misinterpreted. And muteness is more than a physical condition. It always is in the Bible. Muteness is the biblical metaphor for the human condition of voicelessness. The promise of voice is the promise of human enpowerment.

Do we stumble over this miracle story handed to us by the early church? We really ought not to. This miracle has been occurring all around us in this century. The voiceless have started speaking in the larger human community. It's still hard to get used to it when for so long you've been conditioned to expect no significant sound from them. The very word "barbarian" originally meant "one who could not communicate." One who could only say "bar" . . . "bar," one incapable of civilized speech.

How many of you remember the old Tarzan films with Johnny Weismuller or Buster Crabbe? Some of you will remember Saturday afternoon trips to the neighborhood theatre to see those films. Others of you have probably seen the reruns on TV. But for those of us who pre-date television, those films played a different role in our lives. The neighborhood theatre was a powerful instrument for molding our views of others. We learned you could always tell the bad guys; they were the ones in black hats, or else, Mexicans with big mustaches, or Indians. I have a theory from watching the reactions of a certain age group to mustaches and beards. These attitudes were shaped by the media at a certain time. They react adversely because beards in their minds are associated with villainy. I know that my first impression of Africans came through Tarzan films. There was implanted in our young minds the picture of an African as a spear-toting savage whose only speech was an occasional "B'wana" or some unintelligible grunts. There we were, learning about Africa via the neighborhood theatre. Meanwhile, back in Africa, some strange folk called missionaries were working with spittle and whatever else Lord and church provided to inculcate a new consciousness. And before the world knew what had happened, the new representative of the third world was on the scene speaking articulately and persuasively in unexpected power and accent. The third world began to speak; that is the miracle. Go see the excellent film, *Ghandi,* that documents this miracle of our times.

But miracles are not universally applauded. St. Matthew reports Jesus' healing of the dumb man had repercussions in the temple. "By the Prince of Demons he does these things," they said of Jesus. The temple crowd was used to things the way they always had been. Now the balance was being upset. So they started to throw scare stories around, "The Devil is on the loose." When yours has been the only voice doing all the talking for, and the deciding for, and the speaking for and to, you are not disposed to be a listener. And that's how revolutions are born and bred.

But change tack and let Mark's account lead us into other thoughts. Let's not talk about others who are finding their voice today. Let's talk about us in this time and place. Does voicelessness suggest anything about human feelings in these days? Some observers feel there is abroad a feeling of being without voice. Tucked in my note books I found an article entitled "The Bionic Boom." The author was speaking of the popularity of CB radios and the demand for such radios to be equipped with built-in public address systems. He suggested the manufacturers know the human reasons that help sell their product and those feelings are rooted in the sense of voicelessness. Pace, for example, promises "to give you the power to make people listen." The key to this desire for amplification claims the author is the desire to have clout. He went on to say this is the same appeal behind the popularity of the digital watch. These watches have clout; these are the numbers that went to the moon. But more important, one can push a button and the watch obeys. In other words, your children may not listen to you, but your watch will. Not only that, nobody can steal the time off your wrist. Permission must be asked. Then you graciously push the button of your watch and read out the time; there it is, clout.

But put the issue another way. Is there any sense in which we let ourselves become functional mutes in these days? There was a time in our country when people produced their own music and dancing, their own art, even practiced their own medicine. All this was before professionalism occupied the scene. Perhaps we've been awed into silence by another phenomenon of this century, the appearance of the expert, the voice of authority. What is an expert anyway? One definition says that an expert is someone over fifty miles from home. Another definition says that an expert is someone who knows more and more about less and less until finally he knows a great deal about nothing at all. The emergence of these definitions is refreshing. I think we've gone too far with this exaltation of the expert. The aura of the expert has even been invoked to stifle dissent. You've heard the argument "Matters of disarmament are very complicated and we best leave the subject to the experts." Everybody bow in sacred awe.

Currently some of us are working our way through a study of the Gospel of Mark. While we are using a companion commentary, I have stressed over and over again, Mark is prime text, commentary secondary. Learn. Trust your own innate intelligence and powers of observation!

Occasionally I am attracted by a book in the field of theology or biblical studies with an intriguing title. Jackets make great promises. I start reading. The author quotes everyone of established reputation, makes his or her ideas echoes of what someone else has said. It makes for dull reading. One is waiting for the author to break out and say, "But, this is what I think; this is what I say."

And that's the challenge Jesus threw down to disciples, isn't it? Who do men say that I am? *But, "who do* you *say that I am?"*

For those of you who have trouble finding your voice because awe of experts shakes confidence in your own judgment, a story may help. J. P. Berkley, a beloved teacher of the Old Testament, would counsel us: "At clergy meetings colleagues will ask: "Have you read Tillich, Barth, Neihbhur? You'll feel out of it, subdued. Remember this, their names are not written in the New Testament."

Do you remember when all it took to make a great scooter was an orange crate, a two by four, an old roller skate and two sticks? You don't see any homemade scooters like that anymore. You still see an occasional sand-lot baseball game and that's encouraging. We once lived beside a vacant field. The neighborhood youngsters would meet there and play baseball. I used to enjoy the sight, just a group of kids enjoying a game. No screaming coaches, no hysterical parents, no.uniforms, just kids having fun. It didn't have all the polish of Little League baseball or Pop Warner football. Even the clumsy kids got to play. Think about this, "Does the adulation of expertise do something to our own self-confidence and self-expression?" Do we let it make us into functional mutes?

Jesus empowered people, ordinary people. You are somebody. God loves you. Be your own person. I liberate you from the judgments with which others have bound you. "Call no man on earth your Father for one is your father in heaven." These are among the most revolutionary words ever spoken in history.

And this last thought in an even different direction. For some of us, speechlessness is a matter of inner restraint, inhibition. Sometimes the feelings inside of us are all bottled up, but the words to express them just do not come out.

Mr. Bridge is a character created by the novelist Evan Connell. Mr. Bridge is a Kansas City attorney and, in a series of vignettes, the novel illuminates the character of Mr. Bridge. He has trouble at times being articulate about his feelings towards his wife. Often he thought: "My life did not begin until I knew her. She would like to hear this, he was sure, but he did not know how to tell her. In the extremity of passion he cried out in a frantic voice, 'I love you,' yet even those words were unsatisfactory. He wished for something else to say. He needed to let her know how deeply he felt her presence when they were together during the night, as well as each morning when they awoke and in the evening when he came home. However, he could think of nothing appropriate. So the years passed; they had three children and accustomed themselves to a life together, and eventually Mr. Bridge decided that his wife should expect nothing more of him. After all, he was an attorney rather than a poet: He could never pretend to be what he was not."*

---

*From *Mr. Bridge*, by Evan S. Connell, Jr., Copyright Alfred A. Knopf, Inc., New York. Used with permission.

Can you identify with Mr. Bridge? Might you just as well be a mute when it comes to putting feelings into words? I think of a little girl who had just learned to write and was demonstrating her progress to her mother. She wrote a sentence and showed it to her mother. The mother read it and asked, "What happened to the dot over the i?" "Oh, said the little girl. It's still in the pencil." That's the way it is with us sometimes. There is love, joy, warmth inside of us. Words are one way for it to come out into the life of another. Speech is the bridge to human community. It was William Gibson who took the story of Ann Sullivan, Helen Keller's first teacher, and cast it into a play, *The Miracle Worker*. There is a moving scene where Ann places Helen's hand under a stream of pump water, then spells out water on Helen's hand W A T E R, again and again. Then comes the miraculous moment of speech. Helen says her first word "wah wah." Helen Keller later wrote of that experience.

> *"Suddenly I felt a misty consciousness of something forgotten, a thrill of returning thought: And somehow the mystery of language was revealed to me. I knew that wonderful, cool something flowing over my hand. The living word awakened my soul, gave it light, hope, joy, set it free."*

And thinking back on her first full sentence, Helen Keller wrote in her journal:

> *"True, they were broken, stammering syllables, but they were human speech. My soul, conscious of a new strength, came out of bondage and was reaching through those broken symbols of speech to all knowledge and all faith."***

The story of Ann Sullivan going to Alabama to live with Helen Keller has within it echoes of that larger drama of one who came among us, who still comes —

> *To open the eyes that are blind
> the ears that are deaf
> the voices that are silent*

Ephphatha, open up.

**From *The Miracle Worker*, by William Gibson. Copyright by William Gibson. Used with permission.

Lent 5

Mark 8:11-13, 9:14-29

No Sign From Heaven

"Kudzo" is one of my favorite comic strips. The Reverend Will B. Dunn is one of the characters who makes a frequent appearance. Recently Mr. Dunn was in his pulpit thinking some anguished thoughts to himself. "What am I doing here preaching to these people? I have problems of my own. Who am I to talk to them? If I only had a sign. If I only had a sign." In the next-to-last sequence of the strip, a bolt of lightning strikes. The last picture shows Mr. Dunn in his pulpit holding in his hands a sign that says "No Parking." "I don't know what this means," says Mr. Dunn.

That is the trouble with signs from heaven. They can be ambiguous. I'd be worried if I found a sign in the pulpit that said, "No Parking." I can identify with the inner uncertainties of Mr. Dunn. He's honest. I have no patience with the breed of celebrity preachers who, out of the context of affluence, preach a spurious gospel of cheaply won victories, tell us there is no such word as failure in the Christian's vocabulary, and assure us that if we know the trick of thinking right we can make God's power work for us.

That's the way some people were beginning to understand Jesus, as the wonder worker who had the trick to making God's power work. Their attitudes became a problem for him. He was a compassionate man under the constraint of God's love. He responded to human need. His heart went out to others. He healed. Part of the result, in his eyes, was counter productive. Some wanted to make him a celebrity, but he was not on an ego trip. They were looking for a cheap faith. Their ideas were too full of the world's understanding of glory, power, importance. Even the custodians of religion in Israel demanded razzle dazzle signs from him.

Among the most comforting words in the gospel are these: "I believe, help my unbelief." These words of the distraught father of the sick boy reveal the kind of faith Jesus prized and for which Mark pleads throughout his gospel. It's a faith that wavers between trust and doubt. It's a faith that persists and holds on even where it cannot fully understand. It is faith as an act of courage.

Now, I want to do something I have not done before. I want to share with you a dream I had recently even at the risk of raising an eyebrow or two. ("Oh-oh, the preacher is going off the deep end.") The unconscious can play a role in preaching and in coming to grips with the gospel. The late Halford Luccock is the only writer I have encountered who dwells on this.

In going through Mark's gospel I was struck by the fact that in the first part of the gospel, Jesus is surrounded by crowds. In the second part, he stands increasingly alone. My dream fell into that pattern. In the first part I was in a shopping mall in the midst of a bustling crowd. I made my way along and suddenly found myself on an empty street leading into a city. No one was in sight. The city looked dark and menacing. There was a discarded Christmas tree by the curb. I picked it up and carried it along with me. As I walked along the empty street I heard a choir singing "Amazing Grace." I couldn't see them. Their voices came from somewhere up in the tall buildings. Now, I only know for sure the first line of "Amazing Grace." In my dream the choir sang all the verses. A strange light suffused the city with an eerie yet comforting glow.

Reflecting on the dream, I see in it the message of Mark's gospel. The cross means nothing to us until we pick it up, appropriate its meaning into our own lives, and take the leap of faith courageously without benefit of a sign from heaven. It is then when we are on the road that the secret sign is given — a whisper of angel voices, a sense of presence, a strange comfort amid the shadows and ambiguities, a promise of rendez-vous.

Palm Sunday/Passion Sunday

Mark 11:11-23

The Making and the UnMaking of a Church

The Palm Sunday story has all the sounds of a festive occasion — the Hosannahs, The palms, the holiday mood. It was a holiday when he went to Jerusalem. Most probably, it was the feast of tabernacles. But despite the holiday appearances, it's really a sad theme that hovers over the story, the theme of the king who was hailed on one day and rejected on another day.

He came to Jerusalem to make the institutions of Israel people-serving institutions. He came to liberate the truths of God they were betraying in order to share those truths will all the world. He came to remove the barriers to human community erected by piety, patriotism and ethnic pride. He came to put love and servanthood back at the center of religion. What if he had succeeded? What if they hadn't lied, cheated, conspired to get rid of him? What if they had all heeded and acted upon his words? It could have worked out that way. But, it didn't. And that's one of the sad themes that touches this day.

But, there is another sad theme that belongs to this day, the judgment of a great church. This theme Mark makes central in his telling of the story. He focuses our attention on the king who comes and rejects the worship of his people. Mark makes it quite clear to us that the survival of religious institutions is not guaranteed by God. They can become expendable. They can be dismissed from history.

This is the urgent warning sounded in the story of the fig tree and the cleansing of the temple. As is his custom, Mark tells a story within a story that one might interpret the other.

The words of the prophets echo in the story of the fig tree. One can hear the words of Ezekiel that envision the temple as a planting of God on the Hill of Zion.

Thus says the Lord: "I will take a young twig and plant it upon the high and lofty mountain, on the mountain height of Israel will I plant it. That it may bring forth boughs and bear fruit. And, all the trees of the field shall know that I the Lord bring low the high tree, and make high the low tree. Make dry the green tree, and make the dry tree flourish." (Ezekiel 17:22-24) One can also hear the Prophet Jeremiah voicing the impatience and disappointment of God over the fruitlessness of his people.

When I would gather them, says the Lord, there are no grapes on the vine, nor figs on the fig tree; even the leaves are withered and what I gave them, has passed away from them. (Jeremiah 8:13)

Of course, the story of the barren fig tree is shot through with symbolism. That is the obvious intention of Mark. And, of course, we are apt to stumble over this picture of Jesus uttering a curse. This is not the gentle Jesus, meek and mild, remembered from Sunday school days. This is the Lord who comes and calls his people to make decisions that have consequences for good or ill. The temple is an endangered institution. It is vulnerable to the judgment of Christ. If it does not change, it will pass into historical oblivion.

This is an ominous and heavy theme that hangs over Mark's story. Yet, I think it appropriate to look at it. Not just because it is Palm Sunday but because we are getting ready to celebrate an anniversary. In two weeks we will be celebrating the making of a church, our church, Pilgrim Church, a church still in the making. We hope and pray it will continue to be a church in the making, a tender planting that will bear fruit. The memory of the unmaking of a church can be instructive to us, for that too is continuing possibility.

What had gone wrong, so wrong that the temple received the rebuke of Jesus? Simply stated: In his eyes, the institutional structures and practices had outlived their usefulness. They no longer served the truth of God the temple was called to serve. That can happen in any institution. You in business know how some structures, some ways of doing things can become counter productive. You will grasp immediately what Jesus meant when he said you cannot put new wine into old skins. The time comes when you have to decide between what is negotiable and what is not negotiable. The wine is not negotiable. The skins are. They are expendable. The wine is the truth about God and us. The skins are the structures serving that truth.

Jesus was not against structures. He understood their need. The flower children of the sixties did not. You need structure. Can you imagine a river without banks? The result would be chaos. But structures are not ends in themselves.

They had become that in Israel. They had all sorts of practices that made sense sometime in the past — eating Kosher meat, fasting, ritual hand washing before meals, the keeping of special days, and Sabbath do's and don'ts. But these practices no longer served any useful purposes. In fact, they were getting in the way of building human community. So, Jesus challenged every one of them. They were majoring in minors. Big issues and petty issues were getting all confused. That can so easily happen. The story is told of a little boy who was watching a western on TV. His mother came into the room just as the hero was entering a saloon. The little boy said quickly to his mother: "Oh, don't worry, mother, he's not going in there to take a drink. He's just going in to shoot a man."

We who are church professionals are given cause to stop and think as we contemplate Christ judging the worship of his people. Pastors spend a lot of time planning services, thinking about appropriate liturgy, wondering about the proper place for this response or that action. I sometimes wonder just how important it all is. Imagine Jesus coming into our worship service. What would he do? Would he scan the order of service first to see if it was liturgically correct? Then would he read the bulletins and circle all the mistakes? Would he be overly concerned about an occasional sour note or a hymn that was a little schlocky? Or would he be more interested in looking into our hearts to see how we really worship in terms of the love and commitment to him that dwell within us and are revealed by the lives we live. He really wasn't one to major in minors.

There's a story told about the evangelist, Dwight L. Moody. After a service one day, a lady came up to him and said: "Mr. Moody, there were eleven grammatical errors in your sermon today." Moody replied: "Lady, my grammatical knowledge is limited. But what grammatical competence I have has been placed at the service of the kingdom of God. What are you doing with your grammatical knowledge?'' That's the way it goes. One can simply lose sight of the things that are of major importance. At a time in Russia when the peasants were in misery, the archdeacon, Nikon, mounted a crusade. His concern was the sign of the cross should be made with two fingers and not three. Majoring in minors could be one reason another great church went into eclipse. That was happening in Israel and Jesus saw it clearly: "You tithe mint, dill and cumin and neglect the weightier matters of the law.''

But, more that that was going on in the great old temple. Called to serve a great mission. They had subverted that mission to their own ends. Jesus said they had turned the temple into a den of thieves. He was talking about the priests of Israel. You know there are little thieves and big thieves. An old English ditty goes this way:

> *The law locks up*
> *both man and boy.*
> *Who steals the goose*
> *from off the common.*
> *But lets the greater felon loose.*
> *Who steals the common*
> *from under the goose.*

What about those who try to steal a country, or a political system, or a church, or the gospel for the sake of selfish interests, or, in order to build personal empires as can be done today via the electronic church?

It is important we see the issue clearly in the challenge of Jesus to the merchants. The issue has nothing to do with church bazaars. The issue was the Court of the Gentiles, that part of the Temple reserved for Gentiles, that sacred space symbolic of God's purpose to save all people. That is where they had set up shop. They didn't care about having any space to remind them of their world responsibility. They didn't expect the Gentiles, even didn't want them. They had lost the vision of a house of prayer for all peoples. Jesus was infuriated by those, who, in the name of piety, had taken God hostage to ethnic, social, dogmatic, and private interests and erected barriers to human community.

And it's important to understand why the money changers were there. People had to buy animals for sacrifice. Only the bronze temple coin was acceptable. Pagan coins were not. Particularly offensive was the Roman denarius with its image of Tiberius and the inscription: "Tiberius Caesar, Pontifex Maximus." Those coins were circulated through Roman military spending. Piety refused to touch them. So the money changers were there to launder the temple income and make it clean. The set-up was a pious fraud and Jesus couldn't stomach it.

In India a religious cult lives by robbing temples. Pastors of city churches will tell you how valuable churches are today to thieves. But there are other more subtle ways to rob churches. Attitudes can rob churches — rob them of vision, rob them of vitality, rob them of sympathy, rob them of courage, rob them of love. They lied when they accused Jesus of wanting to destroy the temple. *They* were the ones who were destroying the temple.

What else was going on in the temple to contribute to the unmaking of this church? Just this: The clue is in the words of Jesus, "a house of prayer for all people." They had substituted housekeeping for world caring. That can happen. It's a matter of not keeping clear the difference between church work and the work of the church. During the fifties when church buildings were sprouting up all across the country, some accused the church of developing an edifice complex. They felt institutional concerns were usurping the vision of mission.

The charge was not really fair. Visible presence is part of mission. A house of worship says something to a community. And a congregation needs facilities, rooms, skins. On the other hand, it is true institutional preoccupation can eclipse the purpose of the skins. There are churches where cracks in the floor and broken windows can evoke more response than cracked heads and broken hearts.

We have our share of well-preserved historic church buildings in New England. They are beautiful. But one wonders what the priorities are of the congregations housed in those buildings. The story is told of the midwestern grandmother who was on an escorted tour of Westminster Abbey. The guide was describing all the tradition-laden architecture of the Abbey when the little grandmother interrupted him: "Tell me young man, has anyone been saved in here recently?" She asked the right question. What's going on in the lives of people here?

When the country boy disciples of Jesus saw the temple, they were quite impressed: "Look teacher, what wonderful stones, what wonderful buildings." Well, the temple was a splendid sight, covering thirteen acres. Jesus told them not one stone would be left upon another. He said that with a great deal of sadness. Jesus loved the temple. It was precious to him. But the temple was not as precious as the God to whom it pointed. The wine is precious, not the skins. The wine is God, you and me, the people around us, and the glue that holds us together — love, acceptance, commitment, the life we share together. Everything else is skins.

Pilgrim Church was founded in large part by the conviction that community is more important than institution. People with names and faces are more important than statistics. The church is a sheep-fold, not a ranch.

In that reason shines a sense of the wine. We want to keep it and not just among ourselves. What is mission and servanthood, but the extension of mission beyond ourselves?

Well, the old temple fell. In AD 70, the brutal Roman legions destroyed it. It was a traumatic event for Jews and Christians. It marked the final separation of Judaism and Christianity. Some Christians were tempted to gloat over the undoing of the old temple. St. Paul warned them to clean up their own act. "If God did not spare the natural branches, neither will he spare you." And that too is the word Mark speaks to the church in every age.

Maundy Thursday

Mark 8:27-38

Jesus Christ —
and Him Crucified

(This sermon involves the use of art work. Obviously this message cannot be delivered from the pulpit. Select a convenient place where easels can be set up and let the sermon flow in an easy conversational style. Many of the examples used will be found right in the local church. The preacher can either secure copies of the art mentioned, and display it during the sermon, or else adapt this message to art of his/her own choosing).

I am coming down in front of you this evening because I am going to make use of paintings and pictures. Our starting point in Mark's gospel is Peter's confession, a pivotal event in the narrative. Peter acknowledges Jesus as the Christ. Jesus then speaks of his suffering and rejection and is chided by Peter. "Peter took him." Peter presumes to take a teacher's stance toward Jesus. Peter is severely rebuked by Jesus. That word "rebuke" is the same word Jesus uses in addressing demons. That is exactly what was going on. Peter was defining Jesus as the Christ in terms of Peter's own cultural values.

Just how Peter thought of the Christ we cannot be sure. It could have been in ethnic terms, as the Davidic liberator. He could have understood Jesus as a more-than-human wonder worker. We know this image of Jesus was much alive in the first century when Mark wrote. Wonder workers abounded in the first century and many modeled Jesus in that image. I believe Mark was taking aim at a cultural adaptation of Jesus and a style of ministry that resulted.

With the rebuke to Peter the disciples fall back in among the crowd. They have not understood. They are back to square one. Jesus issues his call to crossbearing. Jesus insists that he can be understood only in terms of his confrontation with church and state, his servanthood, his rejection, his suffering. And Mark, by the way he tells the story, underlines that insistence.

This resistance to taking Jesus on his own terms, represented by Peter, is always in the church. We are tempted to take Jesus captive, to make a graven image of him in our own likeness or preference. If you make your own image of Jesus, you can escape having to deal with the real Jesus as he understood himself.

At this point I can best illustrate by way of pictures and paintings. The most popular presentation of Jesus in the church has always been in terms of triumphalism. *[This picture, taken from our church school files shows an ethereal Jesus.]* You will recall paintings you have seen showing a resplendent Jesus victorious in heaven. At the Hospice de Beaune, an ancient hospital in Burgundy, there is a striking example of Flemish art. It broods over the main ward room where the poor who were sick were treated. It shows a severe Christ seated upon the throne of judgment. The graves of earth are opening and some are being consigned to a fiery hell while others are being let into paradise. The departed worthies of church and state are seated near the heavenly judge. This kind of representation of Christ came out of the context of a church that espoused imperial religion with totalitarian assumptions.

Closer to our own times are *[these]* familiar faces of Jesus by Sallman and Hoffman. They are in the triumphalist tradition and reflect the values of nineteenth century liberalism. This is the Gentleman Jesus and we are quite comfortable with these portrayals. In a confirmation class once I asked the young people to comment on these two pictures as compared to Rouault's Head of Christ. All except one opted for either the Hoffman or Sallman. The dissenter said, "Rouault's face of Jesus arouses a reaction in me as I imagine the real Jesus triggered reactions in people who rejected him. I feel Rouault is closer to the real Jesus."

[Here is] a picture of the Laughing Jesus that was popular in the sixties. Does he reflect the success ideal of well-fed suburban youth? Christ can be taken captive just as our understanidng of the church can be taken captive.

[Here, again from our church school files, is] a picture of people

going to church. Note that they are all white and middleclass. *[Here is another.]* There are black people pictured, but all the poeple, black and white, are middleclass. This is not the Jesus who mingled with publicans and sinners and so shocked the piety of the day.

[Here is] a wood print by an artist named Hodges. It shows the minister standing before the congregation. The crucifix has been covered over by a screen with bright flowers on it. The work is entitled, "Deliver Us From Unpleasantness." The cross has been screened out.

Our view of Jesus shapes our understanding of discipleship and mission. The model of the wonder-worker breeds a prima donna style of ministry. The wonder-worker dispenses boons and blessings. Or else he knows a trick way of thinking that puts God's power to work for us. Spurious gospels of cheap victories fit neatly into a success and achievement oriented culture. Outside that milieu they fall to pieces. Can one preach a facile gospel of success in a terminal ward, at Auschwitz, at the massacre sight at Asswan? But there is a Christ who can be proclaimed even in those places. There is the real Jesus who came into this fallen world.

[Here are] two paintings that bring us closer to the real Christ of the real world. One is a traditional crucifixion scene, the other contemporary. In both there are signs of victory and promise, but the wounds of earth are also present.

This has been a limited survey. Who do we say is the Christ? How we answer will shape our style of ministry. My intent has been to engender in you a faith that will hold you when life deals out the worst. Good Friday comes. It comes for each of us. We need more than platitudes and placebos and celebrity smiles. We need the word about the crucified God who comes into our darkness to engender hope at the place where hope runs out.

Good Friday

Mark 15:33-39

The Crucified God

Someone once asked the prima ballerina Pavlova what she meant by a certain dance. She replied: "If I could explain it, I would not have had to dance it."

That is not unlike the conclusion Jesus reached with the disciples who were so slow to understand the things he tried to tell them about his vocation. If words alone would have done the job, he would not have had to live it all out. And Jesus is more than a solitary actor who just happens to arrive on the stage of history.

Mark opens his gospel with words that remind us of the very first words of the creation story in Genesis: "The beginning of the gospel of Jesus Christ, the Son of God." Then Mark quotes some words from the prophets Malachi and Isaiah about the God who comes in history. That is the witness of the scriptures, the God who came. He came with words in the prophets and he came again and again and again. But words alone do not fully illumine the drama of the recurring divine human encounter. God himself decided he cannot say it all with words alone. He put his pathos and feelings into more than words. "In many and various ways God spoke of old to our fathers through the prophets, but now he has spoken to us through a Son." The writer of the letter to the Hebrews said that. And do not get yourself boggled up by that word son. Do not stumble over it. Think of the word not in terms of "being" but of "doing." That's the way the Gospel writers think of it. A true son is one who embodies the character, intent, and purpose of the Father.

This is the confession faith makes as it contemplates the living out of this particular life. "Truly, this man was the Son of God." This man embodied the character, intent, and purpose of God, and the place where faith has to make that confession is at the foot of the cross. But even then faith has to decide whether this was the dying of a misguided fanatic calling for Elijah or whether there is something here that illuminates the ongoing pathos and drama of the divine human encounter.

I want to use again a good Markan technique and tell a story within a story, a story about actions saying more than words can ever say. The locale of the story (and it is a true story) is the ward of a large Veterans Hospital. The patients in this ward were men without arms or legs, men with bodies forever broken. Every now and then celebrities visited this ward, as celebrities are inclined to do. The announcement over the loudspeaker informed them that the visitor on this particular day would be a clergyman, a bishop. Someone was heard to mutter: "Okay, Padre, come on in and show this bunch of crippled guys just what you've got to make such a fuss about, Rev. Celebrity."

Later that day the Bishop came. He didn't look like a Bishop. He didn't even have a clerical collar. He went from bed to bed. He didn't say any inanities or suggest unlikely achievements to the hopelessly lame. He remembered not to try and shake hands with an armless man. Then someone asked him, "Hey, Padre, give us a speech." So he spoke. It was a good talk, graphic, earnest. But with the extra sense every speaker has, the Bishop knew they were listening just because they were a captive audience. So he spoke even more earnestly about Jesus Christ wounded, crossed by the sins of the world and for the sins of the world.

He took as his text the words: "He has no form or comeliness that we should desire him." He told them how God identifies with them. But he still knew they were only listening because they were there. A bed is a bed, and no hope is no hope. Before leaving, he prayed, not one from the prayer book but one from the heart. But even as he said "Amen," he knew this was just another visit. As he was leaving, he paused at the door.

Then he suddenly walked back into the ward as if he had forgotten something. The fact is, he had remembered something. He stood before the men and he started to disrobe. You heard me. He started to undress. He took off his coat and let it fall to the floor. He took off his necktie and shirt. He peeled off his undershirt. The patients were spellbound, for they saw how painful each motion was. Then he took off his trousers, his shorts, his shoes, his socks. And everyone saw plainly that each part of his maimed and deformed body was strapped together by an intricate system of braces, pullies and wires. He stood there a moment, and then slowly began to put his clothes back on. There was silence and the stirring of a deep sense of kinship. When dressed, the bishop walked toward the door. Then before leaving, turned, raised his hand above his head and said: "Now unto him who is able to keep you from falling, and to present you faultless before the presence of his Glory with exceeding joy, to the only wise God our saviour be glory and majesty, dominion and power, now and forever. Amen." Then he left their sight.

That story is suggestive of the larger story of the God who comes among us. Who comes not as a big name, not because he is just making another stop on the celebrity circuit. The God who comes and shows himself to us in all his vulnerability. "And the veil of the temple was rent in two." That's a theological statement. Mark puts it in for the same reason an artist puts a halo in a painting. Mark wants us to know what's going on. That veil hung in the temple. It covered the holy of holies the room no one could enter, only the high priest once a year on the Day of Atonement. The dark room, the place where the inscrutable God dwelt in darkness. Jesus dies, and Mark adds, "The veil of the temple was rent in two." This is the unveiling of God, his disrobing if you will. He is no longer hidden from our view. At that point, where the naked God stands before a naked humanity, we encounter the depth and intensity of the love that could never be revealed by words alone.

It's a love that has been there all the time and has always been there. Somehow the notion was abroad in the church that Jesus died so that we might be forgiven, as if God's anger had to be appeased and someone had to take our punishment for us. God wrote the script for a Passion Play so some transaction involving bloodshed could take place. Some theologians talk like that. Mark doesn't. Neither do Matthew, Luke or John.

Jesus didn't die so God could forgive sins. Jesus died because God does forgive sins. Jesus died because God is merciful and compassionate. Jesus died because God does not respect barriers to human community erected by prejudice, piety, dogma, or ideology. He died because God does love the sinner, the outcast. Jesus was crucified because the ways of God are not the ways of militaristic messianism. They never were and never will be. Jesus died because all those things are so. And that they couldn't take, so they hurt him. We are indebted, not to what they did to Jesus. God does not work through lying, cheating, hurting. We are indebted to Jesus and the truth he came to give us even at the cost of his own life. His life and death are the expression of a redeeming love that has been there all the time and always will be.

His story is like the rings of a tree. Cut the tree and you see the rings, but the rings go all through the tree. You see them only at the place where the tree is cut. The story of Jesus is like that, the glimpse in history that we get of the God who was and is and will be.

And the truths of God for which Jesus stood are the truths of God rejected when he was rejected. They were the truths rejected when the prophets before him were rejected. They are the truths that go on being rejected.

When God created us in his own image and gave us the freedom without which we cannot be human, he gave us the freedom with which we can choose not to be human. When God made us free to trust him and love him, he made us free not to trust him, and not to love him.

Several of us for the past few weeks have been plodding through the gospel of Mark, verse by verse. An observation emerges as one catches a sight of the whole sweep of the story. This Jesus who can command the demons, still the wind and waves, multiply the loaves and fishes, cannot control the response of people. When it comes to people's attitudes toward him, his power is weakness. But his weakness and vulnerability is a peculiar and different kind of power that can evoke and call forth the freely given human response. "Truly, this man was the Son of God." And it was a Roman centurion who said that. A man who couldn't keep his own hands clean, a man who even then was commanding an execution squad. And another man, a member of the court that condemned Jesus, comes out of the shadows and dares to openly go and give the body a decent burial according to Jewish custom. What is Mark saying here? Just this — there is something here, something about his coming this way, that can revive in all of us, our essential humanity. Jew or Gentile, there's something universal here. John said it differently. "In him was life, and that life was the light of men."

And there is something here helping each of us hang on to a faith even in those times when our trust is taking a beating and we experience only the absence of God. At the end, Jesus was engulfed by the reality of his rejection and a sense of the absence of God. "My God, My God, why have you forsaken me?" Yet even then he continued to address God, to cling to him. Even at the point where both thinking and experience have exhausted themselves.

I think again of this bishop standing before the amputees and cripples, a silent witness to them; on the one hand of a faith that hangs on; on the other hand of a compassion that reaches out. I think of that scene and my thoughts are drawn to the crucified God. I told you last week we have to keep the crucified Lord at the center of our faith. I said then to beware of all cheap gospels, all sorts of shallow ideas that avoid the cross, all sorts of glowing rhetoric that is but an echo of the cult of success dressed up to sound like Christianity. None of these cheap gospels will serve you when you come up against the pain and suffering of the real world. Personally, I find only in the gospel of the crucified God, an anchor of sanity.

We live in a world in which each day the papers report some new horror story. How can one handle it? Well, many can't. That's why they numb themselves with chemicals or spin off into cults that are in reality little caves of retreat or sit glued to the unreal world of the soap opera, or give an ear to the optimistic religious medicine man. How can one face the real world? Unless there is something here in this proclamation of the crucified God! Unless there is something here in this world about the sorrows of God, the pathos of God, the love that makes itself vulnerable! Unless there is a loving reality that somehow takes unto itself all the futility and suffering, the death and dying past and present of all who die the death of abandonment, and through its own mysterious chemistry transmutes it into love and hope! Unless all history is an ongoing God event! Unless in the midst of the vicious circles of war, poverty, famine, racism, violence, there is one who we meet in the place of desolation. Unless in the midst of those vicious personal circles of despair, alcoholism, drift, death there is one whom comes with the promise "Here am I, Here am I." The God who comes. The crucified God. And he keeps on coming. The gospel never ends, "Behold, I am going before you into Galilee. You'll see me there. I'm coming."

Easter Day

Mark 16:1-8

Miles To Go and Appointments To Keep

One thing St. Mark does not give us as he concludes his gospel is any sort of ending that could be interpreted to suggest, "and they lived happily ever after." It takes him just eight verses to tell us about the first Easter morning. There is no string of appearance stories as we find in Luke or John. We miss the lofty vision of the exalted Jesus that closes Matthew's gospel. It seems even as Mark affirms the resurrection, it is the absence of Jesus that is highlighted rather than his presence. A certain ambiguity clings to the account. But then the life of faith itself is characterized by ambiguity. There are times when I, for one, am not quite sure just where the Lord is. The very brevity of Mark's account suggests he doesn't want anything to detract from the vision of the crucified Jesus that dominates his gospel. In fact, he is not going to let us forget that our risen Lord is Jesus, who came out of Nazareth and was crucified. Nor does he want us to depend on spectacular signs as a ground for faith.

If anything, Mark wants to keep the faith grounded in the real world. He didn't have much patience with the phony kind of religion that abounded in the Greek world and was even invading the church. Remember, Mark was the first gospel writer, the first one who felt the time had come to get the story straight. It was being embroidered out of shape. Before Mark wrote there were just unconnected Jesus traditions floating around in the church. Collections of miracle stories abounded and these were the stock in trade of preachers who made all sorts of shining promises and who presented Jesus as a divine wonder worker, the agent of a cosmic Santa Claus distributing all sorts of favors and benefits, and, or course, themselves as having some special way of sharing this divine power. The memory of the real Jesus was in danger.

The Greeks, of course, were real pigeons for all sorts of cheap promises and easy answers. Miracle workers were part of their everyday scene. The "theos andres," that's what they were called; religious wonder workers who possessed and dispensed the powers and blessings of the gods.

The Greek mythology that saturated the air paved the way for the wonder worker. Recall the myth of Hercules who went out to do all sorts of daring deeds for the Gods. Or, recall the myth of Ambrosia, the secret drink of the Gods that imparted immortality. The problem in Mark's day was some preachers of the church were adopting the style of the wonder workers and turning Jesus Christ into a cosmic Houdini. Whatever happened to the Jesus who went to the cross, the Jesus who refused to give easy answers or honor cheap faith? (Remember how they taunted, "Come on down from the cross. Then we'll believe. Show us some tricks"?) Whatever happened to the Jesus who spoke to conscience in the name of God? It was time to get the story straight. So, Mark wrote.

But we do not have to be back in the first century to discover the appeal of short cuts and panaceas. The old mythology never really died. It just took new shape and form and became mobile. The traveling medicine show is a firm part of our American tradition.

And the myth promoters are still at work. They know how deeply imbedded is the appeal of the magic solution. The next time you read the carton your milk comes in, note that magic word that is invariably there: "Enriched." Then think of ambrosia, the secret super-charged drink of the Gods. Or think of it when you watch all the ads that promise a new you through some particular product that goes into the mouth. Mouthwash is one example. It's the key to sociability. Chlorophyll used to be the big name and I can never think of chlorophyll without recalling the ditty, "Why reeks the goat on yonder hill/who eats his fill on chlorophyll?" Or, the next time you hear the promise that you can have a white tornado in your kitchen, or a saving visit from the man from Sentry or the man from Glad, think of the story of Hercules, messenger of the Gods, possessor of special powers.

All of this still has its religious side, especially ascendant in the last decade. Think of cultism. "Follow the leader who has that special power or knowledge." Or think of all the "how to be healthy and wealthy" religion saturating the airwaves. I had someone tell me in all seriousness one way to get rich was simply to write on every check you signed, the letters FCT, "from the cosmic treasury." I don't know how that was supposed to work, but I was assured money would start flowing in.

Here is a quotation from a question-and-answer interview with a top woman business owner. It appeared in an issue of the glossy magazine published by one of the leading religious empire builders.

Q. "Are there any secrets to running a successful multi-million-dollar business?"

A. "Yes, our company philosophy is God first."

It all sounds so simple, doesn't it? Brooding over it, I had a thought. You know, we are selling anniversary plates to underwrite the cost of our celebration. Bob Allen tells me that sales are sluggish. Let me suggest to you, Bob, that our marketing procedures could be changed. We might learn from the religious pitch men. First, we shouldn't call them "anniversary plates." We should call them "blessing plates." Second, we shouldn't try to market them in our own church, but on T.V. We would have to put some money up front to buy air time for some programs we could put together. We could call it "The Pilgrim Punch Hour." You'd have to advertise me with some media hype. Perhaps as "the man with God's word for this hour." The sermon would be on some such subject as "The Golden Rule Pays Big Dividends." We would have to get tuxedos and evening gowns for the choristers. I could advertise the blessing plates and say they had been prayed over at Plymouth Rock, the shrine of the Pilgrim Punch Hour. We might embroider a testimonial or two, something like this:

Dear Sir, since the blessing plate has hung on our wall, we won the lottery and paid off our mortgage. Praise the Lord.

The thing about this approach is that it just might work. It was the sage of Bridgeport, Phinnias T. Barnum, who said: "Every crowd has a silver lining." You just have to know how to get at the lining and the cheap faith promise is one way. Yes, the appeal of illusions and easy promises is still around. The political medicine man seeks our votes with glowing promises of a New Deal, a Square Deal, a Great Society. War is invested with messianic significance through slogans that promise a war to end war or a war to make the world safe for democracy or an overkill arsenal to insure security. And now there is a new promise in the air, painless war. Our weapons will intercept their weapons in the air and explode them. The video game, Space Invaders, has been invested with the status of a world vision.

Into this world with its blindness and illusions steps St. Mark to proclaim the crucified and risen Lord, to remind us of him who came out on Nazareth, who still comes with his call to discipleship servanthood, bridge building. Mark steps in not as a spoil sport, but as one who cares deeply, as his Master and our Master cares deeply for us.

Out of my notebook comes this little poem by Stanton Coblenz. It is entitled "The Diplomat."

> He sought to spare their feelings with lies
> Hid truth . . . and built a bubble paradise;
> But dealt with them bruises when the bubble burst
> Harsher than if they'd seen the truth at first. *

In Mark's day, the bubble paradises promised by the wonder workers were beginning to burst and Christians were getting hurt, disillusioned, pained. Jerusalem had been destroyed in a war which failed to deliver on its promises. The empire was turning on the church. Peter was martyred. Paul was martyred. The Christ who was expected to return was not in sight. Cheap faith was crumbling and providing no support. A church that was only an echo of the wider world with its false values of glory and success, its blindness to the things of God, would be a church ill equipped to stand up to the empire or be a humanizing influence in that world.

Only a church under the cross could do that. How Jesus is

---

*From "Diplomat" by Stanton A. Coblentz. Copyright 1963 Christian Century Foundation. Reprinted by permission from the November 20, 1963 issue of The Christian Century.

understood shapes the character of the church. Think of him as a wonder worker and the church becomes just a society of consumers. Think of him in terms of his compassion, his obedience, and his cross and you begin to think of the church as a company called to produce mission and service.

The last line of Mark's gospel is a curious one that has baffled scholars. The women commanded to bring the word of grace to Peter and the others are speechless. Mark says: "They said nothing to anyone for they were afraid."

They were afraid. Well, I can understand that. I run scared a lot of the time. The messenger had said: "Jesus who was crucified is Risen." They knew why he was crucified and so do I. And, if Jesus is risen by the power of God, then that is God's "Yes" to Jesus and God's "No" to everything that put him on the cross. That yes of God says, "Yes, I am a God who forgives." "I do not respect human-made barriers to human community." "The ways of messianic militarism are not my ways." If Jesus is risen, then he was right and to be human means to be human the way he was human. And if I accept his commission, is there a cross in it for me too? Will I be criticized? Called naive, unpatriotic, rejected? I can understand why they were running scared.

They said nothing to anyone. That's strange. Was everything aborted at this point? Is the risen Lord on his way to keep an appointment with disciples who won't show because they haven't heard the news? But Mark is writing in the seventh decade of the first century. We know somebody met someone. Is Mark saying: "Not even our fears will get in the way of the Christ who has called us and wants to keep us?'

There is a phrase in the thirteenth chapter of Mark's gospel that I believe illuminates his strange ending. Jesus is talking about the end of the world. He warns his disciples about the false teachers who could come in his name and work signs and wonders. He tells them even the Romans destroying Jerusalem will not be a sign of the end. War isn't a sign of anything but tragedy. The king does not come that way. Jesus says no one knows the hour of the end. Only God. Jesus says: "The end is not yet." You have miles and miles to go, you've got your work to do and you know what that is. Watch, be ready.

Mark recalled those words especially for the church in the seventh decade of the first century. Jesus had not promised a "They-lived-happily-ever-after" outcome to his ministry. That ministry goes on. He goes on. The Gospel goes on. The church goes on. There would not be regular appearances to buttress faith, but he'd be there with them.

But, Mark also wrote for the church in every age. And through this curious ending, he's put the ball right in our court. Don't wonder whether Peter and the others got the word. That's all back then. You've got the word and the promise. You keep the appointment in Galilee. Where is Galilee? Galilee is wherever Jesus lives and works. He goes on! The Gospel goes on! You go on! Mark told us the coming of Jesus was just a beginning. The phrase he used was "the beginning of the gospel of Jesus Christ." The end is not yet. You've got miles and miles to go and appointments to keep. If you want to see him, you've got to be in motion, up and about your work and you know what the work is. Follow him! You'll see him! Just as he promised in Galilee, in the place of ministry and service.

And since this sermon brings us to the end of a journey through Mark's gospel, it is appropriate to end with an ancient prayer of the church for St. Mark's Day.

> *O Almighty God, who has instructed*
> *Thy holy church with the heavenly*
> *doctrine of thy Evangelist Saint*
> *Mark; give us grace, that,*
> *being not like children carried away*
> *with every blast of vain doctrine*
> *we may be established in the truth*
> *of Thy Holy Gospel; through Jesus Christ*
> *our Lord. Amen*

Bibliography

There is no substitute for reading the text itself. Several varied-paced readings of Mark are a prerequisite for an in-depth study of this gospel. One can profit greatly from keeping a personal journal as one proceeds. A total, disciplined, and prayerful absorption in the gospel itself is a means of enlisting one's subconscious mind in the creative process of sermon preparation. A review of the Corinthian correspondence of Paul will illuminate some of the issues of ministry with which Mark deals.

With the text fully in mind, the next step is to enlist the assistance of competent scholarly research. The following studies were helpful in the preparation of this series:

Achtemeier, Paul J. *Mark. Proclamation Commentaries. Fortress Press,* *Philadelphia. 1975. 122 pages.*

The Proclamation commentaries deserve high marks for quality. Paul Achtemeier gives a concise overview of the style and themes of Mark. The work reflects the new thrusts in Marcan studies.

Martin, Ralph. *Mark, Evangelist and Theologian. Zondervan, Grand* *Rapids. 1972. 240 pages.*

One in a series offering current Evangelical perspectives, this book was a rewarding discovery. The author traces in an objective and scholarly way the history of Marcan studies. This is well done and of much value to the student seeking a crash course.

Mays, James Luther, Ed. *Interpreting the Gospels. Fortress Press,* *Philadelphia. 1981. 306 pages.*

This is a collection of articles that orginally appeared in *Interpretation,* *A Journal of Biblical Studies,* published by Union Seminary, Richmond, Virginia. Studies dealing with the types of Jesus traditions afloat in the church prior to the Gospels were most helpful in suggesting some of the imperatives behind the writing of Mark.

Rhoads, David and Donald Michie. *Mark As Story. Fortress Press,* *Philadelphia. 1982. 159 pages.*

Two colleagues whose field is literature make a significant contribution to the study of Mark via an appreciation of his talent as a superlative and sophisticated story teller.

Rhode, Joachim. *Rediscovering the Teaching of the Evangelists.* *Westminister Press, Philadelphia. 1968. 278 pages.*

This book is basic as an introduction to the emergence of redaction criticism.

Schweizer, Eduard. *The Good News According to Mark.* *John Knox Press, Atlanta. 1970. 395 pages.*

This is a solid commentary that helps create an awareness of the theological perspectives of Mark.

Stagg, Frank. *The Gospel of Mark.* *Protestant Radio and Film Commission, Atlanta.*

These are four taped lectures on Mark available from the Protestant Radio and Film Commission in Atlanta. Frank Stagg, Professor Emeritus of New Testament Studies at Southern Baptist Theological Seminary, is provocative, inspiring, and possessed with much common sense.

Weeden, Theodore J. Sr. *Mark, Traditions In Conflict.* *Fortress Press, Philadelphia. 1971. 182 pages.*

Weeden expounds the unusual and provocative thesis that Mark was engaged in a vendetta against the original disciples. He fails, in my judgment, to sustain his main point, but in the process of his argument he makes a compelling case for issues of ministry dealt with by Mark. These are still live issues within the church.